DICTIONARY

OF SLANG

WORDS

VOCABULARY

BUILDING

MANIK JOSHI

<u>Dedication</u>

THIS BOOK IS

DEDICATED

TO THOSE

WHO REALIZE

THE POWER OF ENGLISH

AND WANT TO

LEARN IT

SINCERELY

<u>Copyright Notice</u>

****

<u>IMPORTANT NOTE</u>

This Book is Part of a Series
SERIES Name: "English Word Power"
[A Thirty-Book Series]
BOOK Number: 28
BOOK Title: "Dictionary of Slang Words"

****

What are "Slang Words"?

Slangs are very informal or specific words that are especially used by a particular group of people and are more common in spoken English. In this book, you will study and learn various common slang words and expressions, the parts of speech they belong to, and their meanings.

absent without leave -- escaped from prison

no go -- a failure; a fiasco

no stress -- *(American Slang)* don't worry

one way pockets -- a miser

COCKNEY RHYMING SLANG

Rhyming slang works by taking a usual or common word and using a rhyming phrase of two or three words to replace it. The second or the last word in the rhyming phrase rhymes with the usual or common word. For instance, we can use the rhyming phrase 'apples and pears' in place of the common word 'stairs'

Apples and Pears -- Stairs

You can say "**Apples and pears** are a key part of the home." [*instead of* "**Stairs** are a key part of the home."]

Note: Sometimes, the last word is dropped in common speech. So, you can also say, "**Apples** are a key part of the home." (We dropped **"and pears"** from the above sentence.)

Cockney Rhyming slang Cockney is a dialect of the English language. **Cockney Rhyming slang** is believed to have originated in the mid-19th century in the East End of London. Traditionally, a cockney is someone who lives in the East End of London.

<u>**INTERNET**</u> <u>**SLANGS**</u> [Most Internet slangs are short forms of phrases but often they cannot be pronounced,]

121 -- One to One

2day -- Today

2moro -- Tomorrow

2nite -- Tonight
4EAE -- For Ever and Ever

Codes Used In This Book:

[adj.] -- adjective

[adv.] -- adverb

[det.] -- determiner

[excl.] -- exclamation

[n.] -- noun

[prep.] – preposition

[v.] – verb

<u>Slang Words -- A</u>

01 -- aardvark [n.] -- *(British Slang)* hard work, unpleasant tasks

02 -- abbess [n.] -- *(British Slang)* a woman who runs a brothel

03 -- about done [adj.] -- *(British Slang)* completed or finished

04 -- about right [adj.] -- *(British Slang)* Slightly drunk

05 -- absotively (adv.) -- *(American Slang)* absolutely, positively

06 -- AC/DC [adj.] -- bisexual

07 -- acid [n.] -- LSD ((Lysergic acid diethylamide), an illegal drug that affects people's minds and causes them to see and hear things that are not really there

08 -- action [n.] -- *(American Slang)* the state of feeling excited

09 -- antifreeze [n.] -- *(American Slang)* liquor

10 -- aries [n.] -- heroin, a drug that has strong side effects

11 -- ashes [n.] -- cannabis or marijuana

12 -- aunt Mary [n.] -- cannabis or marijuana

13 -- axe [n.] -- musical instrument, especially a guitar or saxophone

14 -- axeman [n.] -- a man who plays a musical instrument, especially a guitar or saxophone

15 -- axle grease [n.] -- *(British Slang)* a bribe || *(American Slang)* butter

<u>SLANGS -- IDIOMS</u>

01 -- a / one hell of a … / a / one helluva … -- used for emphasizing what somebody is saying or how good something is

02 -- a bit of all right *(British Slang)* -- a person that you think is very attractive in a physical way

03 -- a bit of rough *(British Slang)* -- a man from a low social class who has a physical relationship with a woman of a higher social class

04 -- a bit on the side *(British Slang)* -- the male or female partner of somebody who is married to somebody else; a steady physical relationship with someone who is not married to you

05 -- a cold day in hell -- the time of occurrence of an event that will never happen

06 -- a grape on the business *(Australian Slang)* **--** a person whose presence spoils things for others

<u>RHYMING</u> <u>SLANGS</u>
(Along with COMMON WORDS, they refer to)

01 -- Acker bilk -- *milk*
Example Sentence: Acker bilk is one of the most nutrient-rich beverages we can consume.

02 -- Adam and eve -- *believe*
Example Sentence: You won't *Adam and eve* what she said about his dancing skills.

03 -- Adam and son -- *done*
Example Sentence: His conviction does not mean justice was *Adam and son.*

04 -- Adam and the ants -- *pants*
Example Sentence: You can shop online for a range of men's *Adam and the ants.*

05 -- after darks -- *sharks*
Example Sentence: After darks commonly lose teeth and replace them over their lifetime.

06 -- airs and graces -- *braces*

07 -- Alan minter -- *splinter*
Example Sentence: He got an *Alan minter* in his finger.

08 -- Alan whickers -- *knickers*
09 -- alderman's nail -- *tail*
10 -- Ali afloat -- *coat*

11 -- Ali Mcgraw -- *straw*

12 -- all night rave -- *shave*

13 -- all time loser -- *boozer*

14 -- almond rock -- *frock*

15 -- almond rocks -- *socks*

16 -- ancient Greek -- *reek*

17 -- Andy Cain -- *rain*

Example Sentence: A yellow weather warning for *Andy Cain* and wind has been issued.

18 -- apple cider -- *spider*

19 -- apple core -- *score* (20 pounds)

20 -- apples and pears -- *stairs*

Example Sentence: We sat on the *apples and pears* in the stadium to watch the match.

21 -- April fool -- *stool / tool*

22 -- April showers -- *flowers*

23 -- army and navy -- *gravy*

24 -- artful dodger -- *lodger*

25 -- Arthur Ashe -- *cash*

26 -- Arthur bliss -- *piss*

27 -- ascot races -- *braces*

28 -- ash and oaks -- *smokes*

29 -- aunt Joanna -- *piano*

30 -- aunt Nell -- *smell*

31 -- auntie dot -- *hot*

Example Sentence: How does the human body react to *auntie dot* environments?

32 -- auntie Ella -- *umbrella*

33 -- auntie lily -- *silly*

34 -- auntie Nellie -- *belly*

INTERNET SLANGS

01 -- **AAF:** As a Friend

02 -- **abt:** About

03 -- **ADAD:** Another Day Another Dollar

04 -- **ADIH:** Another Day in Hell

05 -- **ADIP:** Another Day in Paradise

06 -- **ADN:** Any Day Now

07 -- **ADN:** Any Day Now

08 -- **adr:** Address

09 -- **AEAP:** As Early As Possible

10 -- **AFAIC:** As Far As I'm Concerned

11 -- **AFAICS:** As Far As I Can See

12 -- **AFAICT:** As Far As I Can Tell

13 -- **AFAIK:** As Far As I Know

14 -- **AFAIR:** As Far As I Remember

15 -- **AFAIU:** As Far As I Understand

16 -- **AFAP:** As Far As Possible

17 -- **AFK:** Away From Keyboard

18 -- **AKA:** Also Known As

19 -- **AMA:** Ask Me Anything

20 -- **AMA:** Ask me anything

21 -- **ASAIC:** As Soon As I Can

22 -- **ASAP:** As Soon As Possible

23 -- **ASL:** Age/Sex/Location

24 -- **ASLP:** Age/Sex/Location/Picture

25 -- **ATB:** All the Best

26 -- **ATM:** At the Moment

<u>Slang</u> Words -- <u>B</u>

01 -- babe [n.] -- (a). a word used to address a young woman, your wife or lover to show affection |

02-- babe magnet [n.] -- (a). a man who seems to be very attractive to women | **(b)**. a thing possessed by a man that is perceived to be attractive to women

03 -- baby [n.] -- *(American Slang)* a word used to address a young woman, your wife or lover to show affection

04 -- bad [adj.] -- good or excellent

05 -- bang (v.) -- (of a man) to make a physical relationship with a woman

06 -- beak [n.] -- a person, especially a judge, who is in a position of authority

07 -- beefcake [n.] -- an attractive man with a large and muscular body, especially those that appear in shows and magazines

08 -- Beemer [n.] -- *(American Slang)* BMW car

09 -- bender [n.] -- a short period of drinking a lot of alcohol or taking too much drug for your enjoyment

10 -- berk [n.] -- *(British Slang)* a person that lacks intelligence

11 -- bint [n.] -- *(British Slang)* an offensive way of referring to a girl or woman

12 -- bird [n.] -- *(British Slang)* an offensive way of referring to a girl or woman

13 -- bitch [n.] -- (a). a thing that causes problems, troubles or difficulties | **(b)**. an unpleasant woman

14 -- bitching [adj.] -- *(American Slang)* very good; excellent

15 -- bladdered [adj.] -- *(British Slang)* [not before noun] extremely drunk

16 -- blimey [adj.] -- *(British Slang)* used to express surprise, excitement, alarm or anger

17 -- blow (v.) -- *(American Slang)* to leave a place suddenly

18 -- bog [n.] -- *(British Slang)* toilet/bathroom

19 -- boob [n.] -- a woman's breast

20 -- boss [adj.] -- very good

21 -- bot [n.] *(Australian Slang)* -- a person who gets something from somebody by asking them for it rather than by paying for it | *(British Slang)* -- bottom

22 -- brassed off [adj.] -- *(British Slang)* angry, or annoyed [*synonyms*: exasperated]

23 -- bread [n.] -- money

24 -- bristols [n.] -- *(British Slang)* a woman's breasts

25 -- broad [n.] -- *(American Slang)* an offensive way of referring to a woman

26 -- broad [n.] -- a girl, woman or prostitute

27 -- brown stuff [n.] -- *(British Slang)* excrement

28 -- brown sugar [n.] -- (a). an attractive Black woman | **(b)**. heroin

29 -- brown tongue [n.] -- *(Australian Slang)* a person who treats an influential or important person with special kindness or respect to gain their favor

30 -- brunch [n.] -- a combination of breakfast and lunch, a meal that somebody eats in the late morning [*synonyms*: word, word]

31 -- buff [adj.] -- (b). physically fit, attractive and good-looking with big/huge muscles

32 -- bugger's muddle [n.] -- an absolute mess

33 -- bunger [n.] -- *(Australian Slang)* a firework

34 -- bunk (v.) -- *(British Slang)* British to cheat | *(British Slang)* British to abscond. **|| [n.] --** unfashionable

35 -- buns [n.] -- *(American Slang)* **(a)**. the two sides of a person's bottom; buttocks **(b)**. sanitary towels or tampons **||** *(British Slang) food*

36 -- burnout [n.] -- somebody who is mentally, emotionally or physically exhausted

37 -- burnt girl [n.] -- *(American Slang)* terrible, hopeless, frustrated, tired

38 -- business [n.] -- defecation, hypodermic syringe, prostitution

39 -- business girl [n.] -- *(British Slang)* prostitute

40 -- button-short [adj.] -- intellectually deficient

SLANGS -- IDIOMS

01 -- be up the spout *(British Slang)* -- used to describe something that has completely failed, went wrong, been spoilt or ruined, etc. or is not working

02 -- be gagging for it *(British Slang)* -- to want to have intercourse (bodily activity between a man and a woman)

03 -- be gagging for something / to do something *(British Slang)* -- to be extremely eager to have or do something

04 -- be on the game *(British Slang)* -- having intercourse (bodily activity between a man and a woman) with somebody for money; to be a prostitute

05 -- beat it -- (used in orders) to go away immediately; to leave me alone

06 -- blow/sod that for a lark *(British Slang)* -- used by somebody who avoids doing something because it involves too much effort

07 -- brass monkeys | brass monkey weather *(British Slang)* -- used to refer to extremely cold weather.

SLANGS -- PHRASAL VERBS

001 -- big somebody/something up -- *(British Slang)* to strongly praise or recommend somebody/something, more than is deserved

RHYMING SLANGS

(Along with COMMON WORDS, they refer to)

01 -- babbling brook -- *cook*

02 -- bacon and eggs -- *legs*
Example Sentence: Running may not be the cause of your achy *bacon and eggs.*

03 -- bag of fruit -- *suit*

04 -- bag of sand -- *grand*

05 -- bag of yeast -- *priest*

06 -- baked bean -- *queen*

07 -- baker's dozen -- *cousin*

Example Sentence: She was described by her *baker's dozen* as a woman who loved her family

08 -- bale of straw -- *raw*

09 -- ball and chalk -- *walk*

10 -- bangers and mash -- *cash*

Example Sentence: Bangers and mash is an asset that is in currency form.

11 -- Barnaby Rudge -- *judge*

12 -- Barnet fair -- *hair*

Example Sentence: Barnet fair can fall out for many different reasons.

13 -- barney rubble -- *trouble*

14 -- Barry Crocker -- *shocker*

15 -- basin of gravy -- *baby*

16 -- bat and wicket -- *ticket*

17-- battle cruiser -- *boozer*

18 -- bear's paw -- *saw*

19 -- bees and honey -- *money*

20 -- bees wax -- *tax*

21 -- beetles and ants -- *underpants*

22 -- bended knees -- *cheese*

23 -- betty boo -- *zoo*

24 -- big Ben -- *ten*

25 -- big dippers -- *slippers*

Example Sentence: He is seen wearing a casual shirt and *big dippers*.

26 -- bill Wyman -- *hymen*

27 -- Billy goat -- *coat/throat*

28 -- Billy lids -- *kids*

29 -- bin lid -- *quid*

30 -- bird bath -- *laugh*

31 -- bird lime -- *time* (in prison)

32 -- bird's nest -- *chest*

33 -- biscuit and cheese -- *knees*

34 -- biscuit tin -- *chin*

35 -- bladder of lard -- *card*

36 -- blind mice -- *ice*

37 -- blood and blister -- *sister*

38 -- boat race -- *face*

39 -- bob hope -- *dope/soap*

40 -- bob squash -- *wash*

41 -- bonnie and Clyde -- *snide*

42 -- borrow and beg -- *egg*

43 -- bottle and glass -- *class*

44 -- bottle and stopper -- *copper*

Example Sentence: Bottle and stopper has been mined commercially for more than 5,000 years,

45 -- bottle of porter -- *daughter*

Example Sentence: His wife and he welcomed a *bottle of porter* into the world yesterday.

46 -- bottle of sauce -- *horse*

47 -- bow and arrow -- *barrow/sparrow*

48 -- bowler hat -- *cat*

49 -- box of toys -- *noise*

50 -- brace and bits -- *tits*

51 -- brass band -- *hand*

52 -- brass tacks -- *facts*

Example Sentence: Here are some interesting *brass tacks* about the impact of deforestation around the world.

53 -- bread & jam -- *van*

54 -- bread and cheese -- *sneeze*

55 -- bread and honey -- *money*

56 -- Brenda lee -- *key*

57 -- bricks and mortar -- *daughter*

58 -- Brigham young -- *tongue*

59 -- bright and breezy -- *easy*

60 -- British rail -- *email*

Example Sentence: British rail and calendar tools are essential for business success.

61 -- brothers and sisters -- *whiskers*

Example Sentence: Many animals use *brothers and sisters* to help them find their way and follow their prey.

62 -- brown bread -- *dead*

63 -- brown hat -- *cat*

Example Sentence: Are *brown hats* notorious for their indifference to humans?

64 -- bubble and squeak -- *beak / Greek / speak /week*

65 -- bubble bath -- *laugh*

66 -- bucket and pail -- *jail*
Example Sentence: Those who disobeyed govt. order faced *bucket and pail,*

67 -- buddy holly -- *volley*

68 -- bugs bunny -- *money*
Example Sentence: Take care of yourself; take care of your *bugs bunny.*

69 -- bull and cow -- *row* (quarrel)
70 -- bullock bladder -- *ladder*
71 -- bullock's horn -- *pawn*
72 -- bungle & zippy -- *nippy*
73 -- bunny ears -- *tears*
74 -- butcher's hook -- *look*

INTERNET SLANGS

01 -- b/c: Because

02 -- b/w: Between

03 -- B2K: Back to Keyboard

04 -- B3: Blah, Blah, Blah

05 -- B4: Before

06 -- B4N: Bye for Now

07 -- BBF: Best Friends Forever

08 -- BBL: Be Back Later

09 -- BBS: Be Back Soon

10 -- BBT: Be Back Tomorrow

11 -- BD: Big Deal

12 -- **BF:** Boyfriend

13 -- **BFF:** Best Friends Forever

14 -- **BFN:** Bye for Now

15 -- **BM&U:** Between Me and You

16 -- **BOT:** Back on Topic

17 -- **BRB:** Be Right Back

18 -- **bro:** Brother

19 -- **bt:** But

20 -- **BTA:** But Then Again

21 -- **BTW:** By the Way

<u>Slang</u> <u>Words</u> -- C

01 -- **cack [n.]** -- *(British Slang)* solid waste matter that is passed from the body through the bowels [*synonyms*: dung, excrement] | *(British Slang)* **(v.)** -- to get rid of solid waste from the body through the bowels in somebody's clothes

02 -- **call-girl [n.]** -- prostitute

03 -- **can [n.]** -- **(a)**. lavatory | **(b)**. prison | **(c)**.beer | **(d)**. *(British Slang)* pocket | **(e)**. *(American Slang)* backside | **(f)**. *(American Slang)* strong-box | **(g)**. *(American Slang)* strong-box || **(v)**. *(American Slang)* **(a)**. to put somebody in jail | **(b)**. to hide or suppress something

04 -- **cancer stick [n.]** -- a cigarette

05 -- **candy-ass [n.]** -- *(American Slang)* a timid, cowardly, easily frightened, disgraceful person

06 -- **candyman [n.]** -- *(American Slang)* a person who is the seller of illegal drugs

07 -- **case [n.]** -- **(a)**. mad person | **(b)**. a brothel | **(c)**. *(British Slang)* the last one || **(v)**. to carefully inspect a place to commit robbery

08 -- **cauliflower ear [n.]** -- ear swollen by blows, typically in boxing or rugby

09 -- **chav [n.]** -- *(British Slang)* a low-educated young aggressive person who wears designer clothes and starts fights

10 -- **chickenshit** *(American Slang)* **[n.]** -- Nonsense || *(American Slang)* **[adj.]** -- (of a person) not brave [*synonyms*: cowardly]

11 -- **chillax [n.]** -- to calm down or relax and stop feeling angry or nervous about somebody/something || **(v.)** -- to become calm or relax and stop being angry or nervous

12 -- **chink [n.]** -- **(a)**. a Chinese person | **(b)**. money, change

13 -- **choice [n.]** -- *(British Slang)* something bad

14 -- **chow [n.]** -- *(British Slang)* **(a)**. food [*synonyms*: word, word] | **(b)**. a dog of a Chinese breed with long thick hair, a broad muzzle, a curled tail and a bluish-black tongue

15 -- **chuffing [n.]** -- *(British Slang)* a mild swear word used by some people when they are annoyed

16 -- chug (v.) -- *(American Slang)* to drink all of something quickly without stopping

17 -- chute [n.] -- *(British Slang)* rectum

18 -- civvies [n.] -- (used by people in the armed forces) ordinary or civilian clothes as opposed to military uniform

19 -- Civvy Street [n.] -- *(British Slang)* ordinary or civilian life outside the armed forces

20 -- clam [n.] -- (a). mouth | **(b).** *(American Slang)* a dollar

21 -- clam smacker (n). -- (American *Slang*) lesbian

22 -- clapper [n.] -- tongue

23 -- clean (n). -- (a). innocent | **(b).** not carrying weapons or drugs

24 -- click [n.] -- (a). *(American Slang)* a small group of people spending their time together and disallowing others to join them | **(b).** *(American Slang)* kilometer | **(c).** *(British Slang)* robbery || **(v.) (a).** to have a naturally smooth relationship | **(b).** to be a great success | **(c).** *(British Slang)* to obtain a small amount of money

25 -- cock [n.] -- *(British Slang)* used as a friendly form of address between two people

26 -- cottaging [n.] -- *(British Slang)* the practice of homosexual men looking for partners, in a public toilet/bathroom, for making a physical relationship; homosexual activity between men in public toilets

27 -- cow [n.] -- an offensive word for a woman [*synonyms*: word, word]

28 -- cracker [n.] -- *(American Slang)* an offensive word for a poor, low-qualified white person from the southern US

29 -- crackhead [n.] -- a person who is addicted to the powerful illegal drug crack cocaine

30 -- crappy [adj.] -- extremely unpleasant or of extremely bad quality [*synonyms*: nasty]

31 -- creeper [n.] -- a person who behaves in a weird or very strange way

32 -- croak (v.) -- to breathe your last; to die

33 -- crocked [adj.] -- *(American Slang)* drunk

34 -- cruise (v.) -- to go around in public places with a view to finding a partner for making a physical relationship

35 -- crumpet [n.] -- an offensive way of referring to sexually attractive women

36 -- cut (v.) -- to dilute or adulterate | **[n.] --** (music) a record, album track or musical extract | *(British Slang)* drunk

SLANGS -- IDIOMS

01 -- cop it *(British Slang)* **--** to be punished or treated badly because you have done something wrong | to be killed
02 -- cut a rug -- to dance

RHYMING SLANGS

(Along with COMMON WORDS, they refer to)

01 -- cab rank -- *bank*
02 -- Cadbury's flake -- *mistake*

03 -- Cain and Abel -- *table*
Example Sentence: That *Cain and Abel* was sold at a gain of 500 percent.

04 -- Calvin Klein -- *fine*
05 -- can of oil -- *boil*
114 -- canal boat -- *tote*
06 -- candle wax -- *tax*
07 -- cape of good hope -- *soap*
08 -- captain cook -- *book*
09 -- captain kirk -- *work*
10 -- car and scooter -- *computer*
11 -- cardboard box -- *pox*
12 -- carpet pile -- *smile*
13 -- cat and cages -- *wages*
14 -- cat and mouse -- *house*
15 -- cat's hiss -- *piss*
16 -- chalk farm -- *arm*

17 -- chamois leather -- *weather*

Example Sentence: His departure had already been delayed due to *chamois leather.*

18 -- Charles fox -- *box*
19 -- cheerful giver -- *liver*
20 -- cheese & ham -- *scram*
21 -- cheese and kisses -- *missus*

22 -- cherry hog -- *dog*
Example Sentence: She was seen taking her *cherry hog* for a walk.

23 -- cherry pie -- *lie*
24 -- cherry ripe -- *pipe*
25 -- Chevy chase -- *face*
26 -- chew the fat -- *chat*
27 -- chewy toffee -- *coffee*
28 -- chicken and rice -- *nice*

29 -- chicken curry -- *worry*
Example Sentence: Chicken curry is a normal response to uncertainty.

30 -- chicken oriental -- *mental*
31 -- china plate -- *mate*
32 -- china plate -- *mate*
33 -- Chinese blind -- *mind*
34 -- chips & peas -- *knees*
35 -- chocolate fudge -- *judge*
36 -- clever mike -- *bike*
37 -- clothes peg -- *egg*

38 -- cloud seven -- *heaven*
Example Sentence: Cloud seven is said to be the place where God lives.

39 -- coals and coke -- *broke*
40 -- coat and badge -- *cadge*

41 -- cock and hen -- *ten*

Example Sentence: Here are *cock and hen* questions that we posed to them.

42 -- cock sparrow -- *barrow*

43 -- collar and cuff -- *puff*

44 -- comic cuts -- *guts*

45 -- cooking fat -- *cat*

46 -- cough and drag -- *fag* (cigarette)

47 -- country cousin -- *dozen*

48 -- cows and kisses -- *missus* (wife)

49 -- cream cookies -- *bookies*

50 -- crowded space -- *suitcase*

Example Sentence: Which crowded space suits you depends on the type of trip you're making, among others.

51 -- crust of bread -- *head*

52 -- currant bun -- *(sun, also The Sun, a British newspaper)*

53 -- cut and carried -- *married*

54 -- cuts and scratches -- *matches*

INTERNET SLANGS

01 -- CFY: Calling for You

02 -- CMIIW: Correct Me If I'm Wrong

03 -- convo: Conversation

04 -- CTN: Can't Talk Now

05 -- CU: See You

06 -- CUL: See You Later

07 -- CUS: See You Soon

08 -- cuz: Because

09 -- CWOT: Complete Waste of Time

10 -- CYE: Check Your Email

11 -- CYS: Check Your Settings

Slang Words -- D

01 -- **dash [n.]** -- money, a bribe or tip

02 -- **dead and alive (n).** -- a miserable person

03 -- **dead body (n).** -- *(British Slang)* boring and unsociable person

04 -- **death seat (n).** -- (American and Australian *Slang)* the seat beside the driver of a vehicle

05 -- **def [adj.]** -- very good; excellent

06 -- **dial [n.]** -- a person's face

07 -- **dig (v.)** -- to approve of or like something very much

08 -- **dingbat [n.]** -- *(American Slang)* a person lacking in intelligence

09 -- **dippy (adj).** -- odd, eccentric or crazy, somewhat mad

10 -- **dirty [adj.]** -- using illegal drugs

11 -- **ditz [n.]** -- a crazy, silly, eccentric or lighthearted person

12 -- **dog tag [n.]** -- *(American Slang)* a metal tag that US soldiers wear around their necks, giving its name and owner's address

13 -- **dog's breath (n).** -- a contemptible person

14 -- **dop (v.)** -- to fail a test or an exam | to be unsuccessful in completing a period of study at a school, college, etc.

15 -- **dosh [n.]** -- *(British Slang)* money

16 -- **doss [n.]** -- *(British Slang)* **(a)**. an instance of sleeping in rough accommodation or without a real bed. || **(v.)** -- *(British Slang)* **(a)**. to sleep in rough accommodation or without a real bed | **(b)**. to spend your time without any particular reason, purpose or effort

17 -- **dossy (adj).** -- stupid, simple

18 -- **doubloon [n.]** -- money

19 -- **dough [n.]** -- money [*synonyms*: bucks]

20 -- **dreck [n.]** -- *(American Slang)* something of very bad quality [*synonyms*: rubbish, trash]

21 -- **drongo (n.--** *(Australian Slang)* a person who lacks intelligence

22 -- **dude (n.--** *(Australian Slang)* a man, fellow or guy

23 -- **duds [n.]** -- clothes

24 -- **dump [n.]** -- an act of passing solid waste matter from the body through the bowels

25 -- dweeb [n.] -- *(American Slang)* a boy or a man, who is boring, unfashionable and lacks social skills

SLANGS -- IDIOMS

01 -- do a number -- *(American Slang)* to thoroughly abuse, defeat, humiliate or manipulate somebody

02 -- do a runner -- *(British Slang)* to disappear, escape or run away

RHYMING SLANGS
(Along with COMMON WORDS, they refer to)

01 -- daily mail -- *tale*

02 -- daisy roots -- *boots*
Example Sentence: High-quality *daisy roots* don't have to cost a fortune

03 -- dancing fleas -- *keys*

04 -- Darby and Joan -- *moan*

05 -- David Gower -- *shower*

06 -- day's Dawning -- *morning*

07 -- deep-sea diver -- *fiver* (five-pound note)

08 -- Dennis law -- *draw*

09 -- derby Kelly -- *belly*

10 -- Derry and toms -- *bombs*

11 -- dick emery -- *memory*
Example Sentence: How does your *dick emery* work?

12 -- Dicky bird -- *word*

13 -- dig in the grave -- *shave*

14 -- ding dong -- *song*

15 -- ding dong bell -- *hell*

16 -- dinky doo -- *twenty-two*

17 -- do me good -- *wood*

18 -- dog and bone -- *phone*

Example Sentence: He received an error message stating that his *dog and bone* was already in use.

19 -- dog's eye -- *pie*

20 -- dog's meat -- *feet*

21 -- Donald duck -- *luck*

22 -- donkey's ears -- *years*

23 -- door to door -- *four*

24 -- down the drains -- *brains*

25 -- dribs and drabs -- *crabs*

26 -- duck and dive -- *skive*

27-- ducks and drakes -- *shakes*

28 -- duke of Kent -- *rent*

29 -- duke of York -- *chalk*

30 -- dustbin lid -- *kid*

INTERNET SLANGS

01 -- DIKU: Do I Know You

02 -- DL: Dead Link

03 -- DM: Direct Message

04 -- DND: Do Not Disturb

05 -- DW: Don't Worry

Slang Words -- E

01 -- earache / ear-wigging [n.] -- *(British Slang)* continual gossip, or complain

02 -- ear-banger / ear-basher / ear-bender [n.] -- *(Australian Slang)* a person who talks continually

03 -- earbash (v.) -- *(Australian Slang)* talk continually

04 -- eat crow / eat dirt (v.) -- *(British Slang)* to accept insult without complaining

05 -- electric soup [n.] -- a type of alcoholic drink

06 -- enemy [n.] -- *(British Slang)* the wife

07 -- erase (v.) -- *(British Slang)* to murder

RHYMING SLANGS

(Along with COMMON WORDS, they refer to)

01 -- early hours -- *flowers*

Example Sentence: Most edible flowers are best eaten raw.

02 -- Easter bunny -- *funny*

03 -- egg yoke -- *joke*

Example Sentence: The wrong *egg yoke* at the wrong time can shatter your relationships,

04 -- eggs and kippers -- *slippers*

Example Sentence: You can choose from a wide range of *eggs and kippers* online.

05 -- Eiffel tower -- *shower*

06 -- eighteen pence -- *sense*

07 -- elastic bands -- *hands*

Example Sentence: The priest placed his *elastic bands* on her head.

08 -- elephant's trunk -- *drunk*

09 -- eye lash -- *slash*

INTERNET SLANGS

01 -- EM: Excuse Me

02 -- EOM: End of Message

03 -- EOS: End of Story

04 -- EOT: End of Thread

05 -- ETA: Estimated Time of Arrival

<u>Slang</u> <u>Words</u> -- <u>F</u>

01 -- factory [n.] *(British Slang)* -- **(a)**. a police station | **(b)**. drug-manufacturing place

02 -- fag hag [n.] -- a heterosexual woman who prefers to spend much of her time with homosexual men

03 -- fair shake (n). -- *(American Slang)* a fair deal

04 -- fairy [n.] -- an offensive word for a man, who is attracted to people of the same gender

05 -- fancy woman [n.] -- *(British Slang)* -- a woman of questionable morals; a mistress or prostitute

06 -- fanny [n.] -- *(American Slang)* a person's bottom | *(British Slang))* -- female private parts

07 -- fantod [n.] -- a state of worry or excitement

08 -- filth [n.] -- *(British Slang)* (the filth) -- an offensive word for the police

09 -- freebase [adj.] -- a purified solid form of cocaine (a powerful illegal drug), usually refined by heating it in ether and taken by smoking the residue or inhaling the fumes

10 -- freebasing [n.] -- the activity of smoking or inhaling the freebase (a purified solid form of cocaine (a powerful illegal drug), usually refined by heating it in ether)

11 -- fuzz [n.] -- (the fuzz) -- the police

<u>RHYMING</u> <u>SLANGS</u>

(Along with COMMON WORDS, they refer to)

01 -- faith and hope -- *soap*

02 -- fanny Blair -- *hair*

03 -- far east -- *priest*

Example Sentence: How does a *far east* live his life?

04 -- farmer Giles -- *piles*

05 -- fat and skinny -- *mini*

06 -- fat and wide -- *bride*

Example Sentence: A *fat and wide* is a woman who is about to be married or who is newlywed

07 -- father ted -- *dead*

08 -- fiddle and flute -- *suit*

09 -- field of wheat -- *street*

10 -- fireman's hose -- *nose*

11 -- first aid kits -- *tits*

12 -- fish hook -- *book*

13 -- fisherman's daughter -- *water*

Example Sentence: Up to 60% of the human adult body is a *fisherman's daughter*.

14 -- flounder and dab -- *cab*

15 -- foot pump -- *dump*

16 -- fore and aft -- *daft*

17 -- fork and knife -- *wife*

Example Sentence: He blamed the whole fracas on his *fork and knife*.

18 -- four seasons -- *reasons*

19 -- Francis drakes -- *brakes*

20 -- frog and toad -- *road*

21 -- front door -- *bore*

22 -- fruit gum -- *chum*

23 -- frying pan -- *old man* (husband)

01 -- F2F: Face to Face

02 -- FAQ: Frequently Asked Questions

03 -- FKA: Formerly Known As

04 -- FOAF: Friend of a Friend

05 -- FTL: For the Loss

06 -- FTR: For the Record

07 -- FTW: For the Win

08 -- FWIW: For What It's Worth

09 -- FYE: For Your Entertainment

10 -- FYEO: For Your Eyes Only

11 -- FYI: For Your Information

Slang Words -- G

01 -- gaff [n.] -- *(British Slang)* the house, flat / apartment, etc. to live for somebody

02 -- gagger (n). *(American Slang)* -- a disgusting person or situation

03 -- galoot (n). -- a clumsy person or a person who behaves in a rude or socially unacceptable manner

04 -- gang bang [n.] -- **(a)**. an instance when a number of people make physical relations with each other in a group | **(b)**. the successive sexual assault of one person by several people one after the other | **(c)**. an occasion of violent activity that involves members of a criminal gang || **(v.)** -- **(a)**. to make physical relations with each other in a group | **(b)**. (of a group of people) to have **a** successive sexual assault of one person by one after the other | **(c)**. to be involved in violence as a member of a criminal gang

05 -- gangbanger [n.] *(American Slang)* -- a member of a violent street gang

06 -- gangsta [n.] -- *(American Slang)* a member of a street gang (a bunch of criminals or hooligans)

07 -- ganja [n.] -- a drug in the highly potent form, used mainly for smoking, made from the dried leaves and flowers of the hemp plant, marijuana [*synonyms*: cannabis]

08 -- gay [adj.] -- boring, unfashionable and unattractive

09 -- gear [adj.] -- illegal drugs

10 -- git [n.] -- *(British Slang)* an unpleasant man or a man that lacks intelligence

11 -- glasshouse [n.] -- a military prison

12 -- gnarly [adj.] -- *(American Slang)* **(a)**. (in a positive sense) very good; excellent | **(b)**. (in the negative sense) very difficult or bad; not very good

13 -- gob [n.] -- **(a)**. *(British Slang)* used to refer to a person's mouth in a rude manner | **(b)**. a small amount of a substance that is thick and wet | **(c)**. *(American Slang)* something hard, solid, etc. in a large quantity [*synonyms*:

lump, chunk, pile] || **(v.)** -- *(British Slang)* to blow saliva, liquid, food, etc. out of your mouth; spit

14 -- goof-off [n.] -- *(American Slang)* a lazy person who habitually avoids his responsibility or work

15 -- goolie [n.] -- *(British Slang)* used in a rude manner to refer to a man's testicle

16 -- grass [n.] -- Marijuana

17 -- grok (v.) -- *(American Slang)* to completely understand something using your feelings instead of taking into consideration the facts

<u>SLANGS -- IDIOMS</u>

01 -- get it on (with somebody.) -- *(American Slang)* to have intercourse (bodily activity between a man and a woman) with somebody

02 -- get knotted *(British Slang)* -- a rude way to tell somebody to go away or to show somebody that you are angry with them

03 -- get your kit off *(British Slang)* -- to undress yourself

04 -- get your knickers in a twist *(British Slang)* -- to become angry, confused, upset, or worried about something

05 -- get/have your 'end away *(British Slang)* -- to have intercourse (bodily activity between a man and a woman)

06 -- give/have it large *(British Slang)* -- to engage in activities such as dancing, drinking alcohol, and using drugs to seek pleasure

07 -- go banana -- to become very angry, excited, crazy or silly

<u>RHYMING SLANGS</u>

(Along with COMMON WORDS, they refer to)

01 -- gamma ray -- *stray*

02 -- garden gate -- *late / mate/ magistrate*

03 -- gates of Rome -- *home*

04 -- gay and hearty -- *party*

05 -- George raft -- *draught*

06 -- German band -- *hand*
Example Sentence: Wash your hands to prevent infection.

07 -- gin and tonic -- *supersonic*

08 -- ginger beer -- *queer*

09 -- give and take -- *cake*
Example Sentence: He was looking for the best birthday *give and take* to bake.

10 -- glass of water -- *quarter*

11 -- god forbid -- *kid*

12 -- gold watch -- *scotch*

13 -- grass in the park -- *nark*

14 -- grease and grime -- *time*
Example Sentence: Do they want to improve their *grease and grime* management at work?

15 -- Gregory peck -- *neck*

16 -- grumble & grunt -- *cunt*

INTERNET SLANGS

01 -- GA: Go Ahead

02 -- GAL: Get a Life

03 -- GBTW: Get Back to Work

04 -- GF: Girl Friend

05 -- GFN: Gone for Now

06 -- GFU: Good for You

07 -- GG: Good Game

08 -- GJ: Good Job

09 -- GL: Good Luck

10 -- GM: Good Morning

11 -- GMTA: Great Minds Think Alike

12 -- GMV: Got My Vote

13 -- GN: Good Night

14 -- gr8: Great

15 -- GTC: Got to Go

16 -- GTR: Getting Ready

17 -- GTRM: Going to Read Mail

<u>Slang Words -- H</u>

01 -- half-ass (half-arse) (v.) -- (a). to do (something) with little effort or care

02 -- half-assed (half-arsed) [adj.] -- (a). done without care or effort; not well planned | **(b)**. foolish

03 -- hammered [adj.] -- under the influence of alcohol; very drunk

04 -- handwriting [n.] -- size and appearance

05 -- happy fag [n.] -- a marijuana cigarette

06 -- hard stuff [n.] -- *(British Slang)* strong alcoholic liquor

07 -- hard word [n.] -- criticism, disapproval or rejection

08 -- hay [n.] -- (American *Slang)* marijuana

09 -- headshrinker [n.] -- a psychiatrist

10 -- heap (n). *(British Slang)* **--** an old and unreliable motor vehicle

11 -- heater [n.] *(British Slang)* for a pistol

12 -- heave (v.) *(American Slang)* **--** to vomit

13 -- heaven [n.] -- cocaine

14 -- honk (v.) -- (a). to vomit | **(b)**. to smell very badly

15 -- honky [n.] -- *(American Slang)* an insulting or derogatory word for a white person, used by black people

16 -- hood [n.] -- *(American Slang)* **(a)**. a violent criminal, especially a member of a street gang | **(b)**. a person's own neighborhood

17 -- hooter [n.] -- (a). *(British Slang)* a person's large nose | **(b)**. *(American Slang)* a woman's breast

18 -- hurl (v.) -- *(American Slang)* to vomit

<u>SLANGS -- IDIOMS</u>

01 -- have a dekko (at something.) -- *(British Slang)* to have a look (at something)

02 -- have/take a butcher's *(British Slang)* **--** to have a look at something

RHYMING SLANGS

(Along with COMMON WORDS, they refer to)

01 -- habitual knitter -- *bitter*

Example Sentence: There are four basic tastes: sweet, salty, sour, and *habitual knitter.*

02 -- haddock and bloater -- *motor* (four-wheeler)

03 -- hair gel -- *bell*

04 -- hairy knees -- *please*

05 -- hairy nips -- *chips*

06 -- half-inch -- *pinch*

07 -- ham and cheesy -- *easy*

Example Sentence: It is *ham and cheesy* to get started.

08 -- ham and eggs -- *legs*

09 -- Hampton wick -- *prick*

10 -- Harris tweed -- *weed*

11 -- hay stack -- *back*

12 -- here and there -- *chair*

13 -- herring and kipper -- *stripper*

14 -- herring bone -- *phone*

15 -- hide and seek -- *cheek*

16 -- Hillman hunter -- *punter*

17 -- hit and miss -- *kiss*

18 -- Hobson's choice -- *voice*

Example Sentence: He shouted at the top of his *Hobson's choice.*

19 -- holy friar -- *liar*

20 -- holy ghost -- *toast*

INTERNET SLANGS

01 -- HAK: Hugs and Kisses

02 -- HAND: Have a Nice Day

03 -- HB: Hurry Back

04 -- HBD: Happy Birthday

05 -- HBU: How About You

06 -- HHIS: Hanging Head in Shame

07 -- HRU: How are You

08 -- HTH: Hope This Helps

<u>Slang Words -- I</u>

01 -- ice [n.] -- diamond | **(v.)** -- to kill

02 -- ice cold [n.] -- *(American/Australian Slang)* beer

03 -- ice creamer [n.] -- *(British Slang)* an Italian | *(American Slang)* an occasional drug user

04 -- ice man [n.] -- *(American Slang)* **(a)**. a jewel thief | **(b)**. a professional killer

05 -- idiot box [n.] -- a television set

06 -- inked / inky [adj.] -- intoxicated

07 -- inside job [n.] -- a crime committed against a group, organization, etc. by a person belonging to that place or organization

08 -- itchy [adj.] -- restless, eager

09 -- ivan [n.] -- Russians

10 -- ivories [n.] -- **(a)**. teeth | **(b)**. the keys of a piano | **(c)**. dice | **(d)**. billiard balls

<u>RHYMING SLANGS</u>

(Along with COMMON WORDS, they refer to)

01 -- ice rink -- *drink*

02 -- in and out -- *snout*

03 -- Irish pig -- *wig*

04 -- iron tank -- *bank*

Example Sentence: There is no cap on the transfer of funds to your own accounts within the iron tank.

05 -- itch and scratch -- *match*

06 -- jam jar -- *car*

07 -- jam tart -- *heart*

08 -- jenny lee -- *key*

09 -- jimmy riddle -- *piddle*

<u>INTERNET SLANGS</u>

01 -- IAC: In Any Case

02 -- IC: I See

03 -- ICYMI: In Case You Missed It

04 -- IDC: I Don't Care

05 -- IDK: I Don't Know

06 -- IIRC: If I Recall / Remember Correctly

07 -- IIUC: If I Understand Correctly

08 -- IKR: I Know Right

09 -- ILY: I Love You

10 -- IM: Instant Message

11 -- IMHO: In My Humble / Honest Opinion

12 -- IMMD: It Made My Day

13 -- IMNSHO: In My Not So Humble Opinion

14 -- IMO: In My Opinion

15 -- IMY: I Miss You

16 -- IOW: In Other Words

17 -- IRL: In Real Life

18 -- IS: I'm Sorry

19 -- ISO: In Search Of

20 -- ISTM: It Seems to Me

21 -- ITYM: I Think You Mean

Slang Words -- J

01 -- jack [n.] -- **(a).** nothing | **(b).** police officer | **(c).** informer | **(d).** heroin | **(e).** *(American Slang)* money | **(f).** *(British Slang)* an erection || **(v.)** *(British Slang)* to ejaculate || **[adj.]** *(Australian Slang)* tired

02 -- jacket [n.] -- *(American Slang)* a personal file or dossier; a police record

03 -- jaffa [n.] -- *(British Slang)* a sterile or impotent man

04 -- jam sandwich [n.] -- *(British Slang)* a police car

05 -- jamboree bags [n.] -- *(British Slang)* breasts

06 -- jammed [adj.] -- *(American Slang)* intoxicated

07 -- Jap [n.] -- **(a).** *(American Slang)* a young Jewish girl | **(b).** Japanese person or object

08 -- java [n.] -- *(American Slang)* coffee

09 -- jerry [n.] -- *(British Slang)* **(a).** a German | **(b).** a fire | **(c).** a chamber pot

10 -- Jewish [adj.] -- mean, greedy

11 -- jig [n.] -- *(British Slang)* a lie, a deception, a trick | **(v.)** *(Australian Slang)* to stay away from school without permission

12 -- Jill [n.] -- *(British Slang)* a policewoman

13 -- jim-dandy [n.] -- *(American Slang)* something excellent of its kind

14 -- jism [n.] -- a man's semen

15 -- journo [n.] -- *(British Slang)* a journalist

RHYMING SLANGS

(Along with COMMON WORDS, they refer to)

01 -- Joe soap -- *dope*

02 -- jugs of beer -- *ears*

INTERNET SLANGS

01 -- J/C: Just Checking

02 -- J4F: Just for Fun

03 -- JAM: Just a Minute

04 -- JAS: Just a Sec

05 -- JFY: Just for You

06 -- JIC: Just in Case

07 -- JK: Just Kidding

08 -- JMO: Just My Opinion

Slang Words -- K

01 -- kale [n.] -- *(American Slang)* money

02 -- kaput [adj.] -- Out of order; not working; broken beyond repair

03 -- kazoo [n.] -- buttocks

04 -- kennel [n.] *(American Slang)* a poor-quality house

05 -- khazi [n.] -- *(British Slang)* a toilet

06 -- kick-ass [adj.] -- **(a)**. very aggressive, exciting, powerful or forceful | **(b)**. extremely good and successful || **(v.)** -- to be forcefully impressive

07 -- kitchen police [n.] -- *(American Slang)* military personnel who are assigned to works such as washing utensils, preparing vegetables, etc. in an army kitchen, sometimes as a punishment

08 -- knacker (v.) -- *(British Slang)* **(a)**. to make somebody extremely tired | **(b)**. to break, injure somebody or damage something severely

09 -- knackered [adj.] -- *(British Slang)* **(a)**. extremely tired | **(b)**. so old or broken that it can't be used

10 -- knuckle sandwich [n.] -- a hard punch in the mouth with a fist

SLANGS -- IDIOMS

01 -- kangaroo it (v.) -- *(Australian Slang)* to squat

SLANGS -- PHRASAL VERBS

01 -- knock somebody off -- to kill somebody

02 -- knock something off *(British Slang)* -- to steal something; to steal from somewhere

RHYMING SLANGS

(Along with COMMON WORDS, they refer to)

01 -- kick and prance -- *dance*

02 -- kick start -- *tart*

03 -- kidney punch -- *lunch*

Example Sentence: There are so many *kidney punch* options available to us.

<u>INTERNET</u> <u>SLANGS</u>

01 -- KIT: Keep in Touch

Slang Words -- L

01 -- **lady [n.]** -- cocaine

02 -- **lag (v.)** -- to put in jail for crime; to arrest

03 -- **lagged [adj.]** -- drunk, intoxicated

04 -- **lagging [n.]** -- a period of imprisonment

05 -- **lard (adj).** -- *(British Slang)* fat

06 -- **lard (n).** -- *(British Slang)* a fat person

07 -- **large [adj.]** -- excellent | **[n.]** -- *(British Slang)* one thousand

08 -- **larrup (v.)** -- to beat

09 -- **laughing gear [n.]** -- *(British/ Australian Slang)* mouth

10 -- **laughing juice/soup/water [n.]** -- alcoholic drink

11 -- **leathering [n.]** -- a beating

12 -- **leave lunch (v.)** -- *(American Slang)* to vomit

13 -- **lecky [n.]** -- *(British Slang)* electricity

14 -- **leg-biter [n.]** -- a small child

15 -- **legit [n.]** -- actually, really

16 -- **legless [adj.]** -- very drunk

17 -- **les/lesbo [n.]** -- lesbian

18 -- **lettuce (n).** -- money

19 -- **lid [n.]** -- *(British Slang)* **(a)**. ceiling | *(British Slang)* **(b)**. wig | **(c)**. hat | **(d)**. helmet

20 -- **loony bin [n.]** -- a home or hospital for people who are mentally ill

SLANGS -- IDIOMS

01 -- **large it | large it up** *(British Slang)* -- to enjoy yourself through activities such as dancing, drinking alcohol, and using drugs

SLANGS -- PHRASAL VERBS

01 -- leech off -- to behave like a parasite

RHYMING SLANGS

(Along with COMMON WORDS, they refer to)

01 -- lady Godiva -- *fiver*

02 -- left in the lurch -- *church*

03 -- lemon lime -- *good time*

04 -- lemon squash -- *wash*

05 -- lemon squeezy -- *easy*

06 -- light and dark -- *park*

07 -- lion's lair -- *chair*

08 -- loaf of bread -- *head*

Example Sentence: The *loaf of bread* is part of most animals.

09 -- loop the loop -- *soup*

10 -- Lucy Lockett -- *pocket*

11 -- lump of ice -- *advice*

12 -- lump of lead -- *head*

13 -- lump of school -- *fool*

INTERNET SLANGS

01 -- l8: Late

02 -- l8r: Later

03 -- LDR: Long Distance Relationship

04 -- LFG: Looking for Group

05 -- LFM: Looking for More

06 -- LMA: Leave Me Alone

07 -- LMIRL: Let's meet in Real Life

08 -- LMK: Let Me Know

09 -- LOL: Laugh Out Loud / Laughing Out Loud

10 -- LTNS: Long Time No See

11 -- LTR: Long-Term Relationship

12 -- LYLAB: Love You Like a Brother

13 -- LYLAS: Love You Like a Sister

<u>Slang Words -- M</u>

01 -- mainline [adj.] -- connected with the generally accepted ideas [*synonyms*: mainstream]

02 -- mainline (v.) -- to directly inject an illegal drug into your blood vessel

03 -- moll [n.] -- the female friend or companion of a criminal

<u>SLANGS</u> -- <u>IDIOMS</u>

01 -- make it with somebody (*American Slang*) -- to have intercourse (bodily activity between a man and a woman) with somebody

<u>RHYMING</u> <u>SLANGS</u>

(Along with COMMON WORDS, they refer to)

01 -- mangle and wringer -- *singer*

Example Sentence: She had started her career as a *mangle and wringer*.

02 -- me and you -- *menu*

03 -- merry-go-round -- *pound*

04 -- Mickey bliss -- *piss*

05 -- Mickey mouse -- *house*

06 -- micro chip -- *nip*

07 -- mince pies -- *eyes*

08 -- monkey's tail -- *nail*

09 -- mutt and Jeff -- *deaf*

Example Sentence: Many *mutt and Jeff* people are encouraged to get a cochlear implant.

10 -- **mutter and stutter** -- *butter*

11 -- **mystery bags** -- *snags*

INTERNET SLANGS

01 -- **m8:** Mate

02 -- **MHOTY:** My hat's Off to You

03 -- **MMB:** Message Me Back

04 -- **MoF:** Male or Female

05 -- **MOTD:** Message of the Day

06 -- **MP:** My Pleasure

07 -- **MSG:** Message

08 -- **MSM:** Mainstream Media

09 -- **MU:** Miss You

10 -- **MUSM:** Miss You So Much

11 -- **MYOB:** Mind Your Own Business

Slang Words -- N

01 -- nag pie [n.] -- marriage

02 -- nana [n.] -- *(a)*. banana | *(b)*. *(British Slang)* a fool, an idiot | *(c)*. *(Australian Slang)* head

03 -- nark [n.] -- *(British Slang)* a person who makes friendly relations with criminals or wrongdoers to give the police information about their activities [*synonyms*: informer, spy]

04 -- nasty (n). -- sex organs; intercourse

05 -- natch (adv.) -- exactly in a way that you would expect; obvious [*synonyms*: naturally]

06 -- Neanderthal (n). -- an uneducated thug

07 -- necktie–party [n.] -- *(American Slang)* hanging

08 -- negative chug (v). -- *(American Slang)* to vomit

09 -- net [n.] Internet

10 -- nick [n.] -- *(British Slang)* (the nick) a prison or a police station

11 -- nicker [n.] -- *(British Slang)* a pound (in money)

12 -- nine–to–five [n.] -- a regular, full–time, ordinary employment

13 -- nine–to–fiver [n.] -- an office worker or employee

14 -- ninny broth [n.] -- coffee

15 -- nixie (n). -- nothing

16 -- no-good [adj.] -- [only before noun] (of a person) bad, contemptible, useless or worthless

17 -- noodle (noddle) [n.] -- *(American Slang)* a person's head or brain

18 -- nooky (nookie) [n.] -- sexual activity [*synonyms*: intercourse]

19 -- nosh [n.] -- *(British Slang)* food; a meal

20 -- nosh-up [adj.] -- *(British Slang)* a large meal

SLANGS -- IDIOMS

01 -- not give a stuff *(British Slang)* -- to attach no importance to somebody/something and completely ignore them

02 -- not much cop *(British Slang)* -- not very good; disappointing

<u>**RHYMING SLANGS**</u>

(Along with COMMON WORDS, they refer to)

01 -- near and far -- *bar*

02 -- no surrenders -- *suspenders*

03 -- north and south -- *mouth*

04 -- nose and chin -- *gin*

<u>**INTERNET SLANGS**</u>

01 -- NADT: Not a Damn Thing

02 -- NAGI: Not a Good Idea

03 -- NAZ: Name, Address, ZIP

04 -- NBD: No Big Deal

05 -- NBD: No big deal

06 -- NC: No Comment

07 -- ne1: Anyone

08 -- NM: Not Much

09 -- NNTR: No Need to Reply

10 -- Noob: Newbie

11 -- NOYB: None of Your Business

12 -- NP: No Problem

13 -- NRN: No Reply Necessary

14 -- NSFL: Not Safe for Life

15 -- NSFW: Not Safe for Work

16 -- NTS: Note to Self

17 -- NVM: Never Mind

Slang Words -- O

01 -- Obadiah [n.] -- a domestic fire

02 -- odd-lot [n.] -- a police car

03 -- off (v.) -- to kill

04 -- oik [n.] -- *(British Slang)* a person that belongs to a low social class and is considered rude and unpleasant

05 -- oily [n.] -- a stupid, unsophisticated person

06 -- old bag (n). -- an elderly woman

07 -- old bill [n.] -- a police officer

08 -- old hat [adj.] -- old fashioned

09 -- on spec (idi) -- at a risk

10 -- onion [n.] -- head

11 -- op (n). -- a surgical operation

SLANGS -- IDIOMS

01 -- on the job *(British Slang)* **--** having intercourse (bodily activity between a man and a woman) with somebody

RHYMING SLANGS

(Along with COMMON WORDS, they refer to)

01 -- ocean pearl -- *girl*

Example Sentence: She was trying to find the perfect baby *ocean pearl* name.

02 -- ocean wave -- *shave*

03 -- oily rag -- *fag*

04 -- Oliver twist -- *wrist*

05 -- on the floor -- *poor*

Example Sentence: He is too *on the floor* to buy fruits.

06 -- once a week -- *beak*

07 -- ones and twos -- *shoes*

08 -- orchestra stalls -- *balls* (testicles)

INTERNET <u>SLANGS</u>

01 -- OC: Original Content

02 -- OFC: Of Course

03 -- Oh: Overheard

04 -- OIC: Oh! I See

05 -- OMG: Oh My God

06 -- OMW: On My Way

07 -- OT: Off Topic

08 -- OTL: Out to Lunch

<u>Slang Words -- P</u>

01 -- painful (adj) -- Painful is American slang for bad

02 -- palm oil [n.] -- a bribe

03 -- pants [n.] -- *(British Slang)* something of very poor quality [*synonyms:* rubbish]

04 -- pasteboard [n.] -- a card or ticket

05 -- paw cases [n.] -- gloves

06 -- peck alley [n.] -- throat

07 -- pecker [n.] -- *(American Slang)* the organ on the body of a man or male animal that is used for urinating and intercourse

08 -- pedal music [n.] -- stamping feet

09 -- pedal-pusher [n.] -- *(American Slang)* a cyclist

10 -- pedestals [n.] -- feet

11 -- Pedro [n.] -- Spanish-speaking person

12 -- pelf [n.] -- money

13 -- pen pusher [n.] -- an office worker

14 -- perch [n.] -- *(British Slang)* a bed

15 -- Peruvian poof -- *(British Slang)* a cowardly man

16 -- phat [n.] -- *(American Slang)* highly attractive, pleasing and satisfying; very good

17 -- pig [n.] -- an insulting word for a police officer

18 -- pigsty [n.] -- *(British Slang)* a police station

19 -- pillock [n.] -- *(British Slang)* a silly, incompetent or annoying person

20 -- pill-popper [n.] -- a user of pills

21 -- pipe (v.) -- *(British Slang)* **(a)**. to look at or to watch. | *(British Slang)* **(b)**. to *cry or weep* | *(British Slang)* **(c)**. *to talk* | **pipe [n.] --** *(British Slang)* **(a)**. penis | *(British Slang)* **(b)**. tunnel | **(c)**. vein || **pipe (n)** -- an easy course to do in college

22 -- pisser [n.] -- *(a)*. something annoying or disappointing | **(b)**. toilet

23 -- planted [adj.] -- *(British Slang)* buried

24 -- planting [n.] -- *(British Slang)* funeral

25 -- plat [n.] -- *(Australian Slang)* a silly or foolish person

26 -- plonker [n.] -- *(British Slang)* a foolish, inept or irritating person

27 -- **plop (v.)** -- to defecate
28 -- **plum [n.]** -- *(British Slang)* a fool
29 -- **plumbing (n).** -- *(British Slang)* urinary system
30 -- **pock [n.]** -- a policeman
31 -- **pony [n.]** -- *(British Slang)* **(a)**. £25 | **(b)**. a small measure of alcohol
32 -- **pork barrel [n.]** -- *(American Slang)* the legislator's practice of giving funds for a local project into a budget, especially to win votes; the money that is used in this way
33 -- **porky [n.]** -- *(British Slang)* a false or untrue statement; a lie
34 -- **prawn [n.]** -- a fool, an idiot
35 -- **prez [n.]** -- president

SLANGS -- IDIOMS

01 -- **pedal your dogs** -- *(American Slang)* go away!
02 -- **pull a fast one (on somebody)** -- to deceive somebody through a trick
03 -- **put the frighteners on somebody** *(British Slang)* -- to threaten or frighten somebody to make them do what you want

SLANGS -- PHRASAL VERBS

01 -- **put out (for somebody.)** -- *(American Slang)* to agree to have intercourse (bodily activity between a man and a woman) with somebody

RHYMING SLANGS
(Along with COMMON WORDS, they refer to)

01 -- **pat and Mick** -- *sick*
02 -- **pen and ink** -- *stink*
03 -- **penny-come-quick** -- *trick*

04 -- pig and roast -- *toast*

05 -- pimple and blotch -- *scotch*

06 -- ping pong -- *strong*

07 -- pins & pegs -- *legs*

08 -- pipe and drum -- *bum*

09 -- pipe your eye -- *cry*

10 -- plates of meat -- *feet*

11 -- pleasure and pain -- *rain*

Example Sentence: He is worried about *pleasure and pain* on his wedding day.

12 -- pony and trap -- *crap*

13 -- pope on the rope -- *dope*

14 -- profit & loss -- *boss*

<u>INTERNET SLANGS</u>

01 -- P2P: Person to Person

02 -- PAL: Parents are Listening

03 -- PAW: Parents are Watching

04 -- PIN: Parents in Room

05 -- PLMK: Please Let Me Know

06 -- pls: Please

07 -- PM: Private Message

08 -- POS: Parent over Shoulder

09 -- POV: Point of View

10 -- ppl: People

11 -- PTB: Please Text Back

<u>Slang Words -- Q</u>

01 -- quality [n.] -- *(British Slang)* **(a).** of very good quality; excellent

02 -- queer [adj.] -- an offensive way to refer to a man who is not heterosexual

03 -- queer street [n.] -- bankruptcy

04 -- quod [n.] -- prison

<u>INTERNET SLANGS</u>

01 -- Q4U: Question for You

02 -- qt: Cutie

<u>Slang Words -- R</u>

01 -- rad [adj.] -- *(American Slang)* very good; extremely exciting; awesome

02 -- radical [adj.] -- *(American Slang)* extremely good; excellent

03 -- radically (adv.) -- *(American Slang)* in an extremely good way

04 -- radish [n.] -- a fool or a silly person

05 -- rage (v.-- *(Australian Slang)* to go out and do things you enjoy

06 -- rat-arsed [adj.] -- *(British Slang)* extremely drunk

07 -- ratbag [n.] -- *(British Slang)* an unpleasant, disliked or disgusting person

08 -- reefer [n.] -- a cigarette containing cannabis or marijuana

09 -- retard [n.] -- an intelligent person or a person who has not developed normally

10 -- roach [n.] -- the butt (end part) of a cigarette containing marijuana

11 -- roasting [n.] -- an occasion when a woman has intercourse (bodily activity between a man a woman) with two or more men

12 -- rod [n.] -- *(American Slang)* a small gun

13 -- root (v.-- *(Australian Slang)* to make a physical relationship with somebody

14 -- rooted (adj.-- *(Australian Slang)* **(a)**. extremely tired [*synonyms*: exhausted] | **(b)**. so old, damaged or broken that it can't be used

<u>SLANGS -- PHRASAL VERBS</u>

01 -- rub somebody out -- *(American Slang)* to kill somebody

<u>RHYMING SLANGS</u>

(Along with COMMON WORDS, they refer to)

01 -- rabbit and pork -- *talk*

02 -- rank and riches -- *breeches*

03 -- raspberry ripple -- *nipple*

04 -- rats and mice -- *dice*

05 -- rattle and clank -- *bank*

06 -- reels of cotton -- *rotten*

07 -- roast pork -- *fork*

08 -- rock and roll -- *dole*

09 -- rock of ages -- *wages*

10 -- roller coaster -- *toaster*

11 -- rosy lee -- *tea*

12 -- rub-a-dub -- *pub*

13 -- rubber bands -- *hands*

14 -- rubber glove -- *love*

Example Sentence: Rubber glove has nothing to do with what you are expecting to get.

15 -- ruby Murray -- *curry*

16 -- rusty nail -- *jail*

INTERNET SLANGS

01 -- r8: Right

02 -- RBTL: Read between the Lines

03 -- RIP: Rest in Peace

04 -- RL: Real Life

05 -- ROTFL: Rolling on the Floor Laughing

06 -- rt: Retweet

07 -- RTM: Read the Manual

08 -- RU/18: Are You over 18?

Slang Words -- S

01 -- score (v.) -- (a). (of a man) to have intercourse with a new or desired partner | **(b)**. to purchase or get illegal drugs

02 -- screw-up [n.] -- an occasion when you make a big mistake and spoil something

03 -- scumbag [n.] -- an unpleasant, dirty, objectionable or contemptible person

04 -- scuttlebutt [n.] -- *(American Slang)* stories that are often unkind or untrue, about other people's private lives [*synonyms*: gossip]

05 -- Sheila [n.] -- *(Australian Slang)* a girl or young woman

06 -- shrink [n.] -- a doctor (psychiatrist) who is trained to treat people with mental illness or a scientist (psychologist) who studies the mind and the way that people behave

07 -- shtup *(American Slang)* **[n.] --** an act or instance of making physical relation [*synonyms*: intercourse] **|| (v.) --** to make physical relation with somebody [*synonyms*: intercourse]

08 -- sizzled [adj.] -- very drunk [*synonyms*: inebriated]

09 -- skinful [n.] -- *(British Slang)* an amount of alcoholic drink that is enough to make a person very drunk

10 -- skunk [n.] -- (a). an unpleasant or contemptible person | **(b)**. a strong type of cannabis or marijuana

11 -- skunkweed [n.] -- a strong but poor type of cannabis or marijuana

12 -- slag [n.] -- *(British Slang)* an insulting term for a woman, used to indicate that she has a lot of partners for having physical relations

13 -- slammer [n.] -- (the slammer) a prison or jail

14 -- slapper [n.] -- *(British Slang)* an insulting term for a woman, used to indicate that she has been in a physical relationship with a lot of men; a vulgar or coarse woman

15 -- slash [n.] -- *(British Slang)* (a slash) an act of urinating [*synonyms*: piss]

16 -- smack [n.] -- the drug heroin

17 -- smacker [n.] -- currency of Britain or US; a British pound or US dollar

18 -- smashed [adj.] -- extremely drunk or intoxicated

19 -- soda (n.-- *(Australian Slang)* something easily done [*synonyms*: pushover]

20 -- space cadet [n.] -- a person who behaves strangely and appears to be in his or her own world of imagination

21 -- splitsville [n.] -- the end of a relationship, especially that is romantic or physical [*synonyms*: word, word]

22 -- squaddie [n.] -- *(British Slang)* a new or private soldier; a soldier of low rank in the army

23 -- squeeze [n.] -- *(American Slang)* orange juice

24 -- stiff [n.] -- **(a)**. the body of a dead person | **(b)**. a boring, conventional person

25 -- strewth (exclamation.) -- *(British Slang)* used to express surprise, anger, sadness, disappointment, etc.

26 -- strung out [adj.] -- **(a)**. spread or stretched out into a long line | **(b)**. addicted to or strongly influenced by drugs such as heroin or cocaine

27 -- suck (v.) -- (something sucks) used to say that you dislike something very much because it is of extremely bad quality, taste, etc. or filled with boredom, terrible situation, etc.

28 -- sucker [n.] -- *(British Slang)* used to refer to a particular person or thing for emphasis, in a general way

SLANGS -- IDIOMS

01 -- shut your mouth/face! -- a rude and angry way of telling somebody to stop talking and remain silent

02 -- snuff it *(British Slang)* -- to die

SLANGS -- PHRASAL VERBS

01 -- shack up with somebody | be shacked up with somebody -- to start living or to be living with somebody, without getting married, that you have a physical relationship with

02 -- shoot up | shoot something up -- to directly inject an illegal drug into your blood vessel

<u>RHYMING</u> <u>SLANGS</u>

(Along with COMMON WORDS, they refer to)

01 -- salmon and trout -- *snout*

02 -- satin and silk -- *milk*

03 -- saucepan handle -- *candle*

04 -- sausage and mash -- *cash*

05 -- sausage roll -- *goal*

06 -- scotch mist -- *pissed*

07 -- scotch peg -- *egg*

Example Sentence: The most common scotch peg used today is the hen's scotch peg.

08 -- septic tank -- *yank*

09 -- sexton Blake -- *cake*

10 -- skin and blister -- *sister*

11 -- sky rocket -- *pocket*

12 -- soda roll -- *goal*

13 -- sorry and sad -- *bad*

14 -- Spanish dancer -- *cancer*

15 -- stand to attention -- *pension*

16 -- sticky beak -- *peek*

17 -- stinging nettle -- *kettle*

Example Sentence: A few days ago, I noticed that our *stinging nettle* had started leaking.

18 -- stock and die -- *pie*

19 -- storm and strife -- *wife*

20 -- sugar candy -- *handy*

21 -- sweaty sock -- *jock* (Scottish person)

22 -- Sweeney Todd -- *flying squad*

23 -- syrup of fig -- *wig*

INTERNET SLANGS

01 -- SCNR: Sorry, Could Not Resist

02 -- SEP: Someone Else's Problem

03 -- SFLR: Sorry, for Late Reply

04 -- SFW: Safe for Work

05 -- sis: Sister

06 -- SMH: Shaking My Head

07 -- SO: Significant Other

08 -- SOL: Sooner Or Later

09 -- some1: Someone

10 -- srsly: Seriously

11 -- sry: Sorry

12 -- str8: Straight

13 -- SYS: See You Soon

<u>Slang Words</u> -- <u>T</u>

01 -- ta (excl.) -- thank you

02 -- tackle [n.] -- *(British Slang)* a man's private organs

03 -- talent [n.] -- *(British Slang)* sexually attractive people

04 -- tanker [n.] -- *(British Slang)* a heavy drinker

05 -- tater [n.] -- potato

06 -- team [n.] -- a gang

07 -- teapot [n.] -- *(British Slang) a person who drinks too much tea*

08 -- threads [n.] -- *(American Slang)* clothes

09 -- throw (v.) -- to vomit

10 -- ticker [n.] -- a watch

11 -- tiny [n.] -- *(British Slang)* a small child

12 -- toad (n). -- a liar

13 -- toerag [n.] -- *(British Slang)* an extremely unpleasant, contemptible or worthless person

14 -- top banana (n). -- the leading person

15 -- torch job [n.] -- the crime of deliberately setting fire to a building, vehicles, etc.

16 -- tosh [adj.] -- *(British Slang)* nonsense [*synonyms*: rubbish]

17 -- tosser [n.] -- *(British Slang)* a silly or unpleasant person

18 -- tosspot [n.] -- *(British Slang)* an extremely unpleasant and foolish person

19 -- totty [n.] -- *(British Slang)* attractive women that are thought to be the objects of sexual desire

20 -- toughie [n.] -- a thug

21 -- towel head [n.] -- an Arab

22 -- trap [n.] -- mouth [*synonyms*: gob]

23 -- trip [n.] -- the experience of seeing or hearing things that are not really there that somebody has if they are under the influence of a powerful drug (psychoactive substances)

24 -- twonk [n.] -- *(British Slang)* a foolish person

SLANGS -- IDIOMS

01 -- tie one on *(American Slang)* **--** to get extremely drunk

02 -- turn a trick *(American Slang)* **--** to have intercourse (bodily activity between a man and a woman) with somebody for money

RHYMING SLANGS

(Along with COMMON WORDS, they refer to)

01 -- tea leaf -- *thief*

02 -- tennis racquet -- *jacket*

Example Sentence: He removes his jacket and wraps it around my shoulders,

03 -- these and those -- *toes*

04 -- this and that -- *hat*

Example Sentence: A *this and that* is usually worn out of doors to give protection from the weather.

05 -- tick tack -- *track*

06 -- tit for tat -- *hat*

07 -- toe rag -- *slag*

08 -- tom and dick -- *sick*

09 -- trams and trains -- *brains/drains*

10 -- treacle tart -- *sweetheart*

11 -- trouble and strife -- *wife*

Example Sentence: His *trouble and strife* was raised in a very different environment.

12 -- true till death -- *breath*

13 -- twist and shouts -- *sprouts*

14 -- two and eight -- *state* (of upset)

<u>INTERNET SLANGS</u>

01 -- TBA: to Be Announced

02 -- TBC: to Be Continued

03 -- TBF: To Be Fair

04 -- TBH: to Be Honest

05 -- TC: Take Care

06 -- TFTI: Thanks for the Invite

07 -- TG: That's Great

08 -- TGIF: Thank God It's Friday

09 -- THX: Thanks

10 -- TIA: Thanks in Advance

11 -- TIL: Today I Learned

12 -- TLC: Tender Loving Care

13 -- TMI: Too Much Information

14 -- TTFN: Ta-Ta for Now

15 -- TTYL: Talk to You Later

16 -- TTYS: Talk to You Soon

17 -- Txt: Text

18 -- TYT: Take Your Time

19 -- TYVM: Thank You Very Much

Slang Words -- U

01 -- unhealthy [adj.] -- dangerous to life

02 -- unhip [adj.] -- ignorant or unfashionable

03 -- untogether [adj.] (a). badly organized; incompetent | **(b).** mentally or emotionally unstable

04 -- user [n.] -- a person who uses drugs that are illegal

SLANGS -- IDIOMS

01 -- up the duff *(British Slang)* **--** pregnant lady

RHYMING SLANGS

(Along with COMMON WORDS, they refer to)

01 -- uncle willy -- *silly*

INTERNET SLANGS

01 -- U: You

02 -- U4F: You Forever

03 -- UR: Your

Slang Words -- V

RHYMING SLANGS

(Along with COMMON WORDS, they refer to)

01 -- Vera Lynn -- *gin*

INTERNET SLANGS

01 -- VBG: Very Big Grin
02 -- VSF: Very Sad Face

Slang Words -- W

01 -- **wasted [adj.]** -- strongly affected by the use of alcohol or drugs

02 -- **wazoo [n.]** -- *(American Slang)* a person's bottom (the part they sit on)

03 -- **wedding tackle [n.]** -- *(British Slang)* private parts of a man

04 -- **wedged [adj.]** -- *(British Slang)* wealthy

05 -- **whack (v.)** -- *(American Slang)* to attack and kill somebody

06 -- **white space [n.]** -- free time

07 -- **whitey [n.]** -- (used offensively by black people) a white person

08 -- **wicked [adj.]** -- very good

09 -- **wiener [n.]** -- a word for a man's private part, used by children

10 -- **winker [n.]** -- an eye, eyelash or eyelid

11 -- **wipe-out [n.]** -- failure

12 -- **wise guy [n.]** -- *(American Slang)* a member of the Mafia

13 -- **witchy [adj.]** -- mysterious or weird

14 -- **wonga [n.]** -- *(British Slang)* money, funds or wealth

15 -- **wrecked [adj.]** -- *(British Slang)* [not before noun] extremely drunk

16 -- **wuss [n.]** -- a weak or coward person

SLANGS -- PHRASAL VERBS

01 -- **work somebody over** -- to attack somebody and hit them in order to make them do something such as provide you information

02 -- **wrap up | wrap it up** -- used as an order to tell somebody to stop talking or creating problems, trouble, etc.

RHYMING SLANGS

(Along with COMMON WORDS, they refer to)

01 -- **weakest link** -- *drink*

02 -- weasel & stoat -- *coat*

03 -- weep and wail -- *tale*

04 -- weeping willow -- *pillow*

05 -- whistle and flute -- *suit* (of clothes)

<u>INTERNET SLANGS</u>

01 -- w/e: Whatever

02 -- w/o: Without

03 -- w8: Wait

04 -- WAU: Who are You

05 -- WB: Welcome Back

06 -- WBU: What About You?

07 -- WEG: Wicked Evil Grin

08 -- WFM: Works for Me

09 -- WKND: Weekend

10 -- WOM: Word of Mouth

11 -- WRT: With Regard To

12 -- WUF: Where You From

13 -- WYCM: Will You Call Me?

Slang Words -- XYZ

01 -- yellow boy [n.] -- a gold coin

02 -- yellow-belly [n.] -- a coward

03 -- yenta (n). -- **(a)**. noisy, meddling, shrewish woman | **(b)**. a gossip

04 -- yeti (n). -- *(British Slang)* a primitive, disgusting or silly person

05 -- yo (exclamation) -- (used by young people) hello

06 -- york (v). -- *(American Slang)* to vomit

07 -- yo-yo (n). -- a foolish person who can be easily manipulated

08 -- zec (v.) -- *(American Slang)* to fall asleep, to sleep

09 -- zero [n.] -- a person who is not at all important; an insignificant person

10 -- zero (v.) -- an insignificant person

11 -- zippo [n.] -- nothing

12 -- zonked [adj.] -- [not before noun] -- **(a)**. under the influence of drugs or alcohol | **(b)**. tired out

RHYMING SLANGS

(Along with COMMON WORDS, they refer to)

01 -- yet to be -- *free*

02 -- young and old -- *cold*

INTERNET SLANGS

01 -- Y: Why

02 -- YAM: Yet another Meeting

03 -- YGM: You've Got Mail

04 -- YMMD: You Made My Day

05 -- YNK: You Never Know

06 -- YOLO: You Only Live Once

07 -- YW: You're Welcome

08 -- za: Pizza

09 -- ZZZ: Sleeping

About the Author

Manik Joshi was born on January 26, 1979, at Ranikhet, a picturesque town in the Kumaon region of the Indian state of Uttarakhand. He is a permanent resident of the Sheeshmahal area of Kathgodam located in the city of Haldwani in the Kumaon region of Uttarakhand in India. He completed his schooling in four different schools. He is a science graduate in the ZBC – zoology, botany, and chemistry – subjects. He is also an MBA with a specialization in marketing. Additionally, he holds diplomas in "computer applications", "multimedia and web-designing", and "computer hardware and networking". During his schooldays, he wanted to enter the field of medical science; however, after graduation, he shifted his focus to the field of management. After obtaining his MBA, he enrolled in a computer education center; he became so fascinated with working on the computer that he decided to develop his career in this field. Over the following years, he worked at some computer-related full-time jobs. Following that, he became interested in Internet Marketing, particularly in domaining (business of buying and selling domain names), web design (creating websites), and various other online jobs. However, later he shifted his focus solely to self-publishing. Manik is a nature-lover. He has always been fascinated by overcast skies. He is passionate about traveling and enjoys solo travel most of the time rather than traveling in groups. He is actually quite a loner who prefers to do his own thing. He likes to listen to music, particularly when he is working on the computer. Reading and writing are definitely his favorite pastimes, but he has no interest in sports. Manik has always dreamed of a prosperous life and prefers to live a life of luxury. He has a keen interest in politics because he believes it is politics that decides everything else. He feels a sense of gratification sharing his experiences and knowledge with the outside world. However, he is an introvert by nature and thus gives prominence to only a few people in his personal life. He is not a spiritual man, yet he actively seeks knowledge about the metaphysical world; he is particularly interested in learning about life beyond death. In addition to writing academic/informational text and fictional content, he also maintains a personal diary. He has always had a desire to stand out from the crowd. He does not believe in treading the beaten path and avoids copying someone else's path to success. Two things he always refrains from are smoking and drinking; he is a teetotaler and very health-conscious. He usually wakes up before the sun rises. He starts his morning with meditation and exercise. Fitness is an integral and indispensable part of his life. He gets energized by solving complex problems. He loves himself the way he is and he loves the way he looks. He doesn't believe in following fashion trends. He dresses according to what suits him & what he is comfortable in. He believes in taking calculated risks. His philosophy is to expect the best but prepare for the worst. According to him, you can't succeed if you are unwilling to fail. For Manik, life is about learning from mistakes and figuring out how to move forward.

Amazon Author Page of Manik Joshi:
https://www.amazon.com/author/manikjoshi
Email: manik85joshi@gmail.com

BIBLIOGRAPHY

(A). SERIES TITLE: "ENGLISH DAILY USE" [40 BOOKS]

01. How to Start a Sentence
02. English Interrogative Sentences
03. English Imperative Sentences
04. Negative Forms In English
05. Learn English Exclamations
06. English Causative Sentences
07. English Conditional Sentences
08. Creating Long Sentences In English
09. How to Use Numbers In Conversation
10. Making Comparisons In English
11. Examples of English Correlatives
12. Interchange of Active and Passive Voice
13. Repetition of Words
14. Remarks In the English Language
15. Using Tenses In English
16. English Grammar- Am, Is, Are, Was, Were
17. English Grammar- Do, Does, Did
18. English Grammar- Have, Has, Had
19. English Grammar- Be and Have
20. English Modal Auxiliary Verbs
21. Direct and Indirect Speech
22. Get- Popular English Verb
23. Ending Sentences with Prepositions
24. Popular Sentences In English
25. Common English Sentences
26. Daily Use English Sentences
27. Speak English Sentences Every Day
28. Popular English Idioms and Phrases
29. Common English Phrases
30. Daily English- Important Notes
31. Collocations In the English Language
32. Words That Act as Multiple Parts of Speech (Part 1)
33. Words That Act as Multiple Parts of Speech (Part 2)
34. Nouns In the English Language
35. Regular and Irregular Verbs
36. Transitive and Intransitive Verbs

37. 10,000 Useful Adjectives In English
38. 4,000 Useful Adverbs In English
39. 20 Categories of Transitional Expressions
40. How to End a Sentence

****

(B). SERIES TITLE: "ENGLISH WORD POWER" *[30 BOOKS]*

01. Dictionary of English Synonyms
02. Dictionary of English Antonyms
03. Homonyms, Homophones and Homographs
04. Dictionary of English Capitonyms
05. Dictionary of Prefixes and Suffixes
06. Dictionary of Combining Forms
07. Dictionary of Literary Words
08. Dictionary of Old-fashioned Words
09. Dictionary of Humorous Words
10. Compound Words In English
11. Dictionary of Informal Words
12. Dictionary of Category Words
13. Dictionary of One-word Substitution
14. Hypernyms and Hyponyms
15. Holonyms and Meronyms
16. Oronym Words In English
17. Dictionary of Root Words
18. Dictionary of English Idioms
19. Dictionary of Phrasal Verbs
20. Dictionary of Difficult Words
21. Dictionary of Verbs
22. Dictionary of Adjectives
23. Dictionary of Adverbs
24. Dictionary of Formal Words
25. Dictionary of Technical Words
26. Dictionary of Foreign Words
27. Dictionary of Approving & Disapproving Words
28. Dictionary of Slang Words
29. Advanced English Phrases
30. Words In the English Language

****

<u>**(C). SERIES TITLE: "WORDS IN COMMON USAGE" [10 BOOKS]**</u>

01. How to Use the Word "Break" In English
02. How to Use the Word "Come" In English
03. How to Use the Word "Go" In English
04. How to Use the Word "Have" In English
05. How to Use the Word "Make" In English
06. How to Use the Word "Put" In English
07. How to Use the Word "Run" In English
08. How to Use the Word "Set" In English
09. How to Use the Word "Take" In English
10. How to Use the Word "Turn" In English

****

<u>**(D). SERIES TITLE: "WORDS BY NUMBER OF LETTERS" [10 BOOKS]**</u>

01. Dictionary of 4-Letter Words
02. Dictionary of 5-Letter Words
03. Dictionary of 6-Letter Words
04. Dictionary of 7-Letter Words
05. Dictionary of 8-Letter Words
06. Dictionary of 9-Letter Words
07. Dictionary of 10-Letter Words
08. Dictionary of 11-Letter Words
09. Dictionary of 12- to 14-Letter Words
10. Dictionary of 15- to 18-Letter Words

****

<u>**(E). SERIES TITLE: "ENGLISH WORKSHEETS" [10 BOOKS]**</u>

01. English Word Exercises (Part 1)
02. English Word Exercises (Part 2)
03. English Word Exercises (Part 3)
04. English Sentence Exercises (Part 1)
05. English Sentence Exercises (Part 2)
06. English Sentence Exercises (Part 3)
07. Test Your English
08. Match the Two Parts of the Words
09. Letter-Order In Words
10. Choose the Correct Spelling